# what you left behind

BETHANY A. YATES

to those who love my dark side just as much as my light
and stare in awe as a cycle between them

*when you left*

did the bare branches
beg the leaves to s
                    t
                  a
                 y

abandonment is seasonal

you were mourned long before you died.

*addiction had a way of killing you*

i'm still trying to stomach the lies you fed me from heroin spoons.

*i lost my appetite*

the way you cursed me...
i could have sworn he was your ventriloquist
the way you **slammed** the door...
i could have sworn he was your puppeteer


*like father, like son*

the sound of your voice is absent from my memories. i can't remember hearing it once. i can't envision how your lips formed words or imagine what they would speak of. it's as if the sound waves your throat composed never rippled through my ears; as if your entire life was unintentionally muted over the years. silence splinters my skull and makes my grieving heart ache. this isn't how i imagined your voice would sound or the pain it would create.

*i wish you told me you loved me, brother*

i discovered the birthmark upon your hand as you lay lifeless in your coffin. identical to my own, your death will be forever memorialized in the form of a birthmark. our birthmark.

*we had more in common than i thought*

sometimes i think that planting you six feet underground was the best thing we could have done for you to grow. no matter how much we nurtured you, you wilted before our very eyes. it's natural to mourn your potential and the things you'll miss out on. like watching you grow towards the sky and starting your own garden. but i remind myself that you were an opium poppy among sunflowers and that wasn't going to change. i happily think of how you'll miss out on all the pain of cyclically wilting into a distorted and parched version of yourself. i imagine the devastation of helplessly watching you wither until the ground swallows you whole. i don't know how long i could have watched. three years was already far too heartbreaking.

*i miss you, but i don't want you back*

i don't feel ready to embrace you with open arms when your arms so violently shook as you bellowed death threats to your only son in our front yard. these are the same arms that punched me in the back of the head as i cried at the scene of his car accident when i was fourteen. all of a sudden we're at his funeral six years later and your arms reach out for me lovingly.

*i didn't know they could do that*

rose colored or blood colored
the glasses through which you see
both may feel like love to you
but one feels hateful to me

*domestic violence*

you don't need to be invisible anymore. you're safe now.

*he's gone*

i hate seeing you injure yourself with the same words he
assaulted you with.

*~~mother~~ sand nigger*

abandoned homes
succumb to the nature
that keeps visitors out
and memories hostage
with no chance of renewal
maybe these homes
weren't meant to be

~~homesick~~ *familysick*

for years, nearly empty shells of human beings gathered around the table for holiday meals. as eyes grew hollow, chairs became vacant. tonight, i'm feasting with my demons.

*happy thanksgiving*

i'm grateful to have saved you
even if just for a little while
but now it's time for me to
save myself

*codependent love*

your demons cradle me
with a warmth
as heavenly as hell
on a freezing day

your demons lull me to sleep
on restless nights
so you can direct the villains
of my nightmares

*manipulated into staying*

a comforter
will never comfort me
the way your arms did
when they caressed me
with the warmth of your love

*insomnia*

and to think i had the power
to make your pupil and iris eclipse
whenever  i appeared
or whispered  your name

*now i'm powerless*

your love was not enough
because i needed you
to love me the way i loved you
and you couldn't do that
because momma always said
others don't have a heart like mine

*i felt lonely when i was with you*

when he whispered *i love you,*
what i heard was *you can save me.*

when you whispered *you can save me,*
what i heard was *i love you.*

*i was wrong*

the parts of itself the moon reveals
wade back into the darkness
it calls home

*withdrawal*

i wear yesterday's pain like day old makeup and slept in clothing.

*i'll take them off eventually*

the way the current kisses the shore
and rushes back to its lips each time it leaves
makes me think you'll do the same

*wishful thinking*

i thought we were all flowers in the garden
though all along i've been an insufferable weed
rooting and budding alike, but a nuisance
for i'm not beautiful like the rest of you

*will weeds ever learn to kill themselves?*

a weeping willow, i surrender my leaves as soon as the autumn gusts command me to. people say i'm resilient and strong when my branches begin to sprout after enduring such a devastating winter, but an evergreen is much stronger than i because she protectively cradled her leaves when winter demanded otherwise.

*i had to let you go*

i've spent months trying to erase the love letters i wrote you in number two lead, but there remains faint traces of you, of that love, on this parchment. i've come to realize it will never be perfectly white again, the folds never crisply flat again. i write one for him, one for her, and one for him, but always with a pencil because i know none of them are worthy of the permanency of ink. yet, here i am: a piece of parchment forever altered by sonnets that were intended to be temporary. their remnants will bleed into the love letter i one day scribe in ink.

*each of you will be with me*

*what you left*

it's late september
you plant me indoors
to survive  the winter
yet i still decay
for it's in my nature
to die this way

*tragedy  is genetic*

learning to love you is like
a bird learning to fly
while trapped inside its cage

*daddy issues*

i unwittingly pull myself away from you
but it's not you i'm trying to distance myself from

*daddy issues ii*

no, i don't want to talk. it's not that i don't love you, it's just
that you never taught me how to relate to a man and no
man has ever took the time to teach me how to relate to
them so i don't know how to relate to you. i don't know
what language to speak with both my body and my throat
when you're around. all i know is that there is this gaping
hole inside my chest that was reserved for dad, but you
are misshapen and will never fit in that hole correctly even
if you try. so what's the point? honestly, i don't even
understand the value of having a father because there was
never anything my mother couldn't give me. just like
countless others, i'm the woman without a father and the
emptiness that comes with that label is what makes me
whole. i don't know how to exist any other way. i'm not
sure when i'll be ready. maybe one day i will be, but for
now i will continue to see what you leave on your son's
gravestone to know that you're still alive.

*forgive me father*

our romance was a disguise for the series of clinical trials i
underwent. i thought your love would cure me, but
infatuation was simply a placebo effect. poor treatment
outcomes led to the frequent tweaking of your medicinal
compounds. there was a lot of trial and error, trial and
error. you were always on trial when there was the
slightest error. i understand now that this is incurable. this
chronic emptiness is incurable. maybe you thought i'd cure
you too. i'm sorry for poisoning you.

*the hole daddy left*

getting over him is like picking scabs
in the process of healing
wounds become exposed again

*why can't i let myself heal?*

i am the glass that delivers sunlight into your dark home. i am the glass you bring to your lips for intoxication. please be mindful that glass is dangerous when it shatters and when i shatter i'll make you bleed. all i ask is that you handle me carefully.

*difficult to love*

i have dreams of dying
but don't confuse dreams
with nightmares

*depression*

i need a bullet to soothe this itch in my brain.

*suicidal again*

years of diet pills for breakfast
couldn't suppress my appetite for love
years of starvation for lunch
never gave me fulfillment
years of laxatives for dinner
didn't purge this repulsion
i can't stomach to look at myself
i can no longer tell our voices apart
even when i was gilded bones
i was worthless

*i blame you, you, and you*

you admire the vibrant petals coiled so beautifully that they became a universal representation of love. i admire the many thorns that formed after each heartbreak she had. like the awfully sharp ones near her blossom that grew after she no longer wanted to feel the slightest touch of a man. these thorns shriek *don't touch me* and *i'll hurt you before you can hurt me.* they armor the entirety of her stem where people have tried to sever her from her home, knowing that she is nothing without her roots. this is the way, the only way she knows she is safe. but how lonely it is to never be vulnerable.

*safety is isolating*

i have an obsession with writing lists of people i think would attend my funeral. i scribble and i write and i scratch off names until something feels right, but it never does. i list them from most to least likely to attend based on the excuses they make in my head. i crumble the paper and throw it away. i start all over by rewriting the same names. i ask my friends if they still love me because somehow by saying *yes* they are rsvping to the event of the year. so i add their names to the guest list, but i know they won't make it here. i think samantha would like to come, but she has to work that day. marcus will bluntly say *i'm sorry, but that doesn't sound like much fun.* christine contemplates attending, but decides she doesn't like me all that much anymore. my first love, he resents me for breaking his heart and calls me a whore. my guest list is empty. it's empty. it's always fucking empty… except for my father. he would be there. the same father i've been estranged from since the age of fourteen. he will attend because his favorite party favor is pitty.

*my pen is running out of ink*

i would rather remain safe on land
listening to the ocean through a shell
than to drown while embracing it

*love*

i grew because
the pain you caused me
was the nutrient-rich dirt
that needed to be paired
with my mother's sunbeams
and my own willingness
to water myself.

*pain can be nurturing*

the most beautiful thing about the sun
is how its light projects onto the moon

the most beautiful parts of me
are the most beautiful parts of you

*mother*

i know we're on a joyride but you need to know that my mind operates as two radio stations competing for the same frequency. show me what love is by attentively deciphering each word i speak through the screaming static. show me patience by giving me a few more miles to decide which wave to settle on.

*i promise i'm worth listening to*

the words cling to the freckles on my lips
their clammy hands unintentionally slipping
into the air, one by one in the form of a stammer
until they fall freely like bombs

*i will no longer be silenced*

i began this year
ridding the shelves
of your remains
so that i have room
to collect new things

*moving on*

you tell me you're the lead singer of a band. you ask *what do you do?* i tell you i'm a social worker. you enthusiastically ask *so you help people?* i respond *yeah, don't you?*

*music saves lives*

my affection for you
like a cherry blossom tree
quickly abounded  with pink petals
which soon fell and sprouted leaves

*infatuation*

the way the passionate sun and tranquil ocean
yearn to collide at the seam of the horizon
resembles the gravitation our hearts felt
seconds before our fingers entwined
and the eager vult of lust that settled
in our stomachs as our lips brushed for the first time

*i want to submerge my soul into yours*

let's say that we each consist of a unique concoction of
liquids that are then evaporated  into what we call souls...
if that's the case, you and i - our souls
they were made the same, darling.

*there's  something about you*

how lucky i am
that out of billions of souls
i'm the one who gets to inhale the air
that once belonged to your lungs


*your existence gives me hope*

like the moon
you control my tides
you make me low
you make me high

*i can't help but gravitate toward you*

all stars are radiant, but you'll forever be my north star.

*finding you is finding home*

for years, my guilty pleasures consisted of things associated with "womanhood."  i will now simply call them *pleasures,* for i choose not to feel guilty for being feminine.

*romance novels*

when i think of him i see a gentle hand extended out to meet mine. we clumsily dance on hardwood floors as we giggle off-beat to the melodies of 60s rock n' roll. we get lost in the woods on rainy days to replenish our souls and reconnect with our mother nature that concrete estranges us from. he has a smile so kind it spreads to his eyes when i send him letters thanking him for being my best friend. he buys me plants instead of cut flowers because he knows i like to nurture something hopeful. he rubs my back when anxiety leaves me spineness. he understands that sometimes the world is just too much for me to handle so we stay in bed and read poetry to each other until one of us falls asleep. if he's first, i'll continue to read love poems aloud in hopes that i am writing the scripts of his dreams.

*my future feminist lover*

i am human
with the complexities
of the universe within me
please don't belittle the
significance of my existence
to the words "cool" or "pretty"
when i hold inside
extraordinary miracles
and endless mysteries

i possess the stars
upon which you gaze
and countless poets fixate
i guide people home while
holding philosophers hostage
in their inquisitive mindstates
i sustain
lives you don't even know exist
and those you don't appreciate

*i'm not a photo prop*

our minds alter three-dimensional objects to fit our own two-dimensional perspectives by labeling the moon "full" without acknowledging that a whole other side exists. we aren't aware of the beauty that lies in the depths we neglect for the sake of cognitive efficiency.

*we do this to people*

i cultivate life and am trusted to cradle the dead.

*being called "dirt" was never an insult*

you are a house with all the lights on. you can't light up the
world, but you can lighten the world of those who pay you
a visit.

*you're welcome here*

you say i'm naive, but in wisdom lies my understanding
that dirty hands are no less worthy than those that are
clean.

*unconditional*

you told me you feel like just another star. we always
talked about how beautiful the night sky is but not how
numbing it must feel to realize there are countless stars
just as beautiful as you. you confessed to me that you feel
inferior. i was confused because here i thought you were
as significant as the moon, constantly comparing himself
to the magnificent beams the sun projects... thinking you
were falling short. i repeatedly reminded you that you're
magnificent in your own way and i told you and told you
and told you why i prefer your light over the sun's. that
wasn't enough for you. i don't know what decides who gets
to be the sun or the moon or the billions of stars... but now
i know that you don't care about being any of those. but
you'll forever be more than just another star.

*i don't know how to help you, but i'll try*

how do i convince you of your worth when your body was currency for drugs at such a young age? it's instilled in you that you're only as good as pussy and cocaine.

*you are everything and more*

with their bodies also died
your hope that they will one day love you

i hope you can hear the love in my silence

*foster child*

we eagerly plant the seeds
we hope grow into beautiful blossoms
but those already sprouting
shrivel from our neglect

nurture *them*
and watch our garden flourish

*foster children*

the flowers fragilized by our scrutiny
sprout through the concrete ceilings
thoughtlessly constructed above them

the weeds we expel from our yards
stand defiantly in gardens
to resist the gentrification of their homes

nature constantly raises its voice
over the silence we enforce
are you listening?

*there's nothing natural about oppression*

she was irrelevant
the second he was assigned
a **primary** color
and she
~~a secondary~~
~~a tertiary~~
some other color

*why can't we all be primary colors?*

my heart stirs thinking about how a masterpiece was once
a blank canvas; the way two interwoven souls were once
lonesome strangers. how this bare paper is now clothed in
an array of words that never existed until this very
moment. how in the womb, there was silence and then
there was a heartbeat.

*all beautiful things were once nothing*

i'm still struggling with what you left behind
but look how i transformed coal into diamonds
and how i help others do the same

www.ingramcontent.com/pod-product-compliance
Lightning Source LLC
Chambersburg PA
CBHW060350050426
42449CB00011B/2916

# Pragmatic Wisdom Vol. 7

Stoic Lessons on Money and Things

James Bellerjeau

A Fine Idea

# Contents

# Why Do Anything? An Introduction to the Stoic Lessons

D ear friends. Join me on a journey to discover what it means to live a good life. Our inspiration in this quest is Seneca's Moral Letters to Lucilius, revisited and revised for our modern times. The search for what it means to live a good life was not new in Seneca's day, and it will not be old when we are all long gone.

Although these are not Seneca's letters, they honor both his wisdom and his instructions for new students. That is, we should grapple with deep thoughts and make our understanding of the truth personal.

Because no one has a monopoly on the truth, we can each contribute to the puzzle. **The reason to do anything is to answer a question that has not been answered, or at a minimum to answer it for yourself.**

In answering life's deepest questions, would it not be foolish for us to pass by the foundational stones laid by the great thinkers who labored before us? Seneca himself in search of inspiration says in his Letter 2:

> I am wont to cross over even into the enemy's camp, — not as a deserter, but as a scout.

Let us all be avid scouts of the great thinkers, seeking out their every camp with the mindset of anthropologists unearthing meaning from among the ruins. Although Seneca's words have been mined by many for centuries, each generation keeps turning up gemstones.

Thus, with this series of Pragmatic Wisdom for Busy People, let us polish old stones to show them in a new light, and in washing off the mud and debris, reveal what fresh reflections may appear.

Be well.

PS — You can read each of the volumes independently, as it suits your time and your interests. Dedicated readers will find, however, that their understanding of each volume will increase upon reading further volumes. The sincere student may therefore wish to have the full set of Stoic letters: Pragmatic Wisdom for the Sincere Student.

Chapter Two

# On Wealth

Once one's feet are stuck on the path to wealth, the scantest few manage to pry themselves from it

T he ties that bind us to bad habits are no less restrictive for being attractive at first glance. The one whose arms are bound by golden chains is no freer than the one in iron shackles.

I am talking about the seductive charms of money, and they have led more from the path of wisdom than any siren song did sailors to their deaths.

"Surely" you say, "I am entitled to take care of myself and to ensure that I have enough to live on." If ever a paving stone belonged on the path to hell, dear reader, it would be this intention.

I grant you that it is suitable and even beneficial that you provide for yourself, and do not need to rely upon the charity of strangers. When you are paid for your toil, you learn the value of work and equally the value of leisure.

Both work and leisure are gifts, and both deserve our deepest contemplation.

But once one's feet are stuck on the path to wealth, the scantest few manage to pry themselves from it. For if a little money is good, more money must be better. But you already know from my earlier letter, that a desire that can never be satisfied is not a true desire.

Plug your ears, then, to the siren song of wealth, but leave open your mind to the alms of philosophy. A true understanding of what it means to live a good life will help you avoid this false temptation.

I was pleased to discover that we have more modern-day Stoics among us than many realize, and it seems that some lessons have made their way safely down the ages.

Though they do not call themselves Stoics, the FIRE movement contains kindred spirits. I refer to "Financial Independence Retire Early," of which we have several different schools of thought. They differ in the sense of how much money the practitioner saves, how much they spend, and what they do with their time.

For our purposes, the operative word for all students is this: Independence. Each works towards passing the test of being in control of their time, and of not relying on others for their contentment or fortune.

However financial independence is defined by each, the FIRE adherent knows that attachment to things impedes progress. You need few possessions to acquire that most valuable thing: Self-possession. Do not spend your time earning money but spend your money to earn yourself time.

Also, who is to say that you would not learn more from dealing with adversity, i.e. by being poor, than you would by never having to deal with want?

To give your mind leisure, do not accumulate things, whether because you cannot afford them, or you have trained yourself not to acquire them. The less you have, the less you worry about. No one will try to take your possessions if you do not have any. Nor will you spend any time worrying about maintaining them.

When your possessions number more than you can hold in your hand, you must worry about how you will carry them about or keep them safe. Here is our old friend Thoreau saying it as he does best:

> Simplicity, simplicity, simplicity! I say, let your affairs be as two or three, and not a hundred or a thousand; instead of a million count half a dozen, and keep your accounts on your thumb-nail.

Now, dear reader, let me caution you as you make your own calculation of how much your independence is worth.

Whatever number you have set for yourself as being enough to allow you to start to live purposefully, it is very likely too high. People today live lives of luxury unimaginable to those of just a few generations back, never mind those stretching back thousands of years.

Lest you think I exaggerate to make my point, let me describe for you a result the Swiss bank UBS found when they surveyed the most successful savers. Across every wealth group, from the mere millionaires to the mega-rich, UBS discovered what we already know: that standard of living expectations increase in line with wealth.

- Those with $1 million felt they would be satisfied with $5 million.

- Those with $5 million thought they could make do with $10 million.

- And those few to have amassed $10 million felt that their way of life would be secure with $25 million.

Like the rabbit leading on the greyhounds, the benchmark moves without the chaser noticing. For it is never the amount as such that makes you feel secure, but the feeling of accumulating more.

Just as a dinner guest shows their appreciation in advance by bringing their host a small gift, I have an offering for you:

> To be content with little is difficult; to be content with much, impossible.

This wisdom comes to us from the pen of Austrian author, Countess Marie von Ebner-Eschenbach. She was born of a Baron, lived in a castle, and was surrounded by libraries of books.

The Countess knew of riches both material and immaterial. It is to our benefit that she placed greater weight on the latter.

Be well.

# Chapter Three

# On Deprivation

## You do not need what you think you need to be happy, because all you need is within you

Another New Year's Day, which means another spate of New Year's resolutions. We promise ourselves that we will change in the new year. The tight waistband of our favorite jeans, the low step count on our Fitbit, the exercise equipment collecting dust in the corner, all that will be different now.

If you were here, dear reader, I would happily listen to your recommendation. Should we be resolute in our retiring ways, or join the crowd in making resolutions? When everyone around us declares their good intentions, what misers are we to withhold our contribution to a more hopeful future?

If all eyes around us turn towards the sky, only a few can keep their gaze on the ground. We are social animals, and to go against the herd is to go against our very humanity.

I know that you are up to the test I will put to you now. Do not be about the setting of annual resolutions, if these be expressed in the form of a goal you wish to achieve. Goals are but wishful thinking.

Better orient yourself along the right path, and follow a system designed to move you in the direction of your choosing. You will arrive in places beyond what you could have imagined using mere goals.

If you have a resolution, let it be this: You will learn to develop new habits, by taking a small thing and practicing it daily for two weeks. In that time, you will either adopt your new habit with relative ease or determine that it is not the one for you.

No need for self-doubt. There are many paths leading to good outcomes, and you will simply choose another. Not the goal, mind you, but merely the path along which you will walk.

What you will learn from learning to adopt habits is that habits are everything. And how wonderful that, despite being so foundational, habits are disarmingly easy to form.

Do you wish to be content with what you have? Practice going without and do so as often as you feel your resolve weakening.

For all those who think "But I need to travel in Business Class, or I will suffer most grievously on the flight" I say this:

- Put yourself happily in the back of the plane, one row from the restrooms.

- What are eight hours when you have a good book to distract you?

- Should I have lost a moment's peace worrying about being a few meters further back in the same plane?

- Am I not especially ridiculous when I imagine the anguish of those who sit one cabin ahead of mine when *they* contemplate the luxuries being lavished on the lucky few in First Class?

- And even those elite are secretly irked by the thought that flying private is so much more civilized.

Better yet, make your vacation one in which you do not set foot in an airport. Let your feet do the work and take a walk to a nearby scenic viewpoint.

For nothing more than the trouble of walking out your door, you can attain peace of mind for no price. A walk in a forest salted with birds is better than any time spent in a concrete jungle, with only the outraged honks of taxis to serenade you.

The lesson you are reinforcing as a diligent student is that you do not need what you think you need to be happy because all you need is within you. When you deprive yourself of things, particularly of comforts, you weaken their power over you. And such is the power of comforts that it leads many to lives of discomfort for fear of losing them.

Not you. By going without, you learn not to fear privation. Besides learning the nature of which things are worth fearing and which are not, you learn not to take for granted that which you have.

After you have been cold and thinly dressed, wet and without an umbrella, hungry and without food, then truly do you become a connoisseur of a warm, dry room and simple food.

When you have trained yourself to be happy with the most basic of nature's offerings, then you have learned to live true to yourself. Happiness never lies in external things, and if it takes our depriving ourselves of things to relearn this lesson, then better for us to cast off all possessions than be weighed down by the slightest of them.

My finger hovers over the send button. "Not without another installment payment on your account," you say. I call on the fortune of the Buddha to help pay this week's debt:

> Holding on to anger is like grasping a hot coal
> with the intent of throwing it at someone else;
> you are the one who gets burned.

The wisdom here is apparent to everyone who has felt anger and been fortunate enough to have it fade away. Some spring repeatedly to anger at the slightest provocation. Anger is satisfying to give vent to because it drives out reason. You are no longer responsible for thought, you are spurred to violent action, be it words or deeds.

You do not wish to be someone who gives up their reason so readily, for this too is habit-forming.

Self-possession means more than not needing things. Self-possession means keeping a tight grip on your reason and not letting anyone or anything external hijack it from you.

Though you may safely cast all else aside, your mind is the one possession you do not make better by depriving yourself of it.

Be well.

# Chapter Four

# On Things of Lasting Value

Not all appreciate that hard work and sacrifice are not just the price for rewards, but a necessary precondition for valuing them

"Not another sermon" you say. "I have heard you preach to others, but do you practice your own lessons? Are you so advanced that you have endless time to pass on your wisdom to those less learned?"

I do not pretend to point out the mote in my brother's eye while ignoring the beam in my own. Consider that I am trying to describe a landscape that I see but dimly, and that by comparing notes with my fellow observers, we each gain a sharper view of its contours.

You are thus my sounding board for good sense. Though I may be just talking to myself, putting my thoughts into words still helps me understand the message.

I tell you one lesson that I must practice and practice, and hence I preach it to myself as often as to others: I shall seek an end to my wants before I come to my own end. As often as I banish wants, still they sprout anew like perennials each spring.

"What harm," I muse, "in this small indulgence? I can afford it, and truly there may be no consequence for my weakness of the moment."

But what a tiny bounty this small pleasure buys, when compared to the erosion of my foundation of self-possession and well-ordered thought! What an unfair trade to grab onto a momentary enjoyment and let go of long-term contentment.

For though the pleasure is fleeting, the memory of it remains. And the memory is not of the enjoyment but of my lapse, or as the saying goes: Act in haste, repent at leisure. With each slip, my footing grows less stable, until I am scarcely able to stand without support.

Contrast this with the memory of virtuous decisions resulting from clear thinking. Rather than death by a thousand cuts, each of these decisions can be safely savored in leisure. They represent a fortification of the soul and not an assault.

Standing firm is the only way to continue to stand firmly, and thus the only path to lasting value is to be true to your values.

There are more obstacles in our path than aids, dear reader, even though it appears that the opposite is true. Consider:

- We live in an age when virtually all knowledge is available at our fingertips, courtesy of Google. The instant a thought or question arises in your mind, you can slake your thirst with a search.

- How many drink deeply enough to fully quench desire, instead of sipping at the sources of wisdom? Though they have been handed the keys to all the libraries of the world, they cannot unlock wisdom.

There have never been more well-informed idiots who know all of the facts and none of their implications.

I put it down to instant gratification. Not only do we feel entitled to satisfy our every want, but what we think we deserve we want right now.

The worst thing you can do with a child is to satisfy their every want, for then they never learn the difference between wants and needs. Are we to be spoiled children into advanced age?

Not all appreciate that hard work and sacrifice are not just the price for rewards, but a necessary precondition for valuing them.

- If I give you something for free, and you have invested no effort in obtaining it, you will value it as highly as any other common thing you can pick up off the ground.

- Because free and easy are today within short reach, few grasp past them to the costly and the challenging.

But if we wish to ensure our safe passage, the hard way is where our path lies. The longer we toil upwards, the greater will be our reward.

The joy that comes from mastering your thoughts is not only the greatest possession, it is the one that cannot be taken from you by another.

I pay now my debt and take my leave:

> The greatest wealth is to live content with little,
> for there is never want where the mind is satisfied.

This comes courtesy of Lucretius, and you marvel at the many routes by which I return to this point.

That is because it is a road you must travel down before you are safe to venture further on. It is also the road to which all others eventually return.

I would have you hear this lesson until it becomes second nature, and you are a safe navigator for yourself and others.

Be well.

# Chapter Five

# On the Meaning of Life

How do we find meaning? By learning to identify all those things that are meaningless, and serve only to weigh us down

S o, I understand your friend is trying to convince you he has figured out the meaning of life.

I recommend a healthy skepticism towards anyone who says they have it all figured out. Exercise particular care with the ones who are selling you a simple solution.

Do you know how rare it is that a person becomes truly enlightened, in the sense of the Buddha or the Dalai Lama? A person who puts their worldly cares behind them and lives a life of joy and compassion?

Perhaps we see signs of it in children. This transcendence is so seldom achieved in adulthood, and so striking when we do find ourselves in its midst, that you will have no trouble mistaking the practitioner for the master.

"My friend is calm and composed" you say, "when others are incensed by small things."

You can observe a cobra from a distance every day and never see it bare its fangs. Until you do. Perhaps it is simply that your friend has not been sufficiently provoked.

Do not be impressed by a person who remains calm when there has been no disturbance. The fact that others are disturbed by small things tells us nothing.

"He condemns politicians who abuse their power, who tend to themselves rather than their constituents."

This says nothing of his true nature, dear reader. For among all those who shrink from the whip, there are but few who would not themselves wield it willingly if the whip should fall into their hands.

The only thing preventing the average person from becoming tyrants themselves is they lack the means to implement their whims. Situations make most people who they are, and it is exceedingly uncommon for a person to make themselves in spite of their limitations.

Though your friend is unlikely to be a guru, if for no other reason than he professes himself as such, there is no shame in being a practitioner.

We are all pilgrims walking the same path and the value for most of us is in the progress we make. Point yourself in the right direction and take a single step, and you have advanced farther than those who run a thousand miles aimlessly.

How do we find meaning? By learning to identify all those things that are meaningless, and serve only to weigh us down:

- public opinion and trends;

- fashion, fame, and fortune;

- anger, envy, and longing.

Note how fickle these things are, and how insubstantial. Though you cannot see them or hold them in your hand, still they are the heaviest of burdens.

With each of these chains we shrug from our shoulders, our load becomes lighter, and our steps more carefree. Satisfaction and joy lie along this path, and the cost to us is giving up things that require us to pay a price, whether in money, time, or attention.

For everything we plan to seek in life, let us first understand the cost to obtain it. Naval Ravikant shows wisdom when he says:

> Desire is a contract you make with yourself to be unhappy until you get what you want.

What is keeping you unhappy? What you want. What do you want? ... Happiness

We do not want things. We want what we think those things will bring us. No matter how eagerly we sought a possession or a promotion, notice how quickly they start to lose their luster the moment we attain them.

- The new car becomes a used car the instant you drive it off the lot.

- The new phone is soon outshone by a rival as sure as the sun will rise tomorrow.

- The big new office that comes with the big new job is quickly filled with the big new problems that you now feel weighing you down.

To make yourself unhappy by wanting things that will not make you happy is not a recipe for success. Let me end again with Lucretius because it bears repeating:

> The greatest wealth is to live content with little,
> for there is never want where the mind is satisfied.

Our most important possession is our self-possession, and once having taken ownership of this, you have all that you need for a meaningful life.

Be well.

# Chapter Six

# On Class and Philosophy

## Philosophy holds out to us the exact same opportunity, regardless of birth, gender, class, or wealth. Truly the way is open to all

Y ou say that you come from humble origins, that your family was lower middle class at best, as if this had anything to do with your ability to mine your reason and become truly rich in happiness!

Philosophy cares not a bit for your social class.

Though your family may be rich or impoverished in money and circumstance, we are each born with the same inalienable rights: Life, liberty, and the pursuit of happiness.

Think how much better your situation is today than humankind throughout most of history, a third or more of whom toiled in slavery. To become wealthy and powerful was the province of kings and generals, and even these could never rest easy because they could lose everything in a moment's weakness.

Today we are born free, and we are free agents, able to direct our attention where we would like and reap the consequences of our actions. That which we create with our own hands and by our own effort belongs to us, which none can take without due process of law.

If you wish to climb the ladder of social mobility, dear reader, there is no better time to be clutching the rungs of progress than today.

Your own career bears out the proof of what I say. Though you were born into poverty and obscurity, you have risen to your current position of prominence through your own hard work.

It is your own efforts you should applaud, for which of your ancestors labored alongside you in getting you to where you are today?

Go back down the family tree of mankind, and you see that we all share a common ancestor. Do you want noble blood in your family? Look but a bit further and you will find your kingly kinship.

But take little comfort from your royalty, because you will also find all manner of rogues and scoundrels among these relatives, who wreaked havoc and destruction on humanity.

If you wish to bask in the reflected glory of others' deeds, you must also accept to be doused in shame and remorse from their misdeeds.

No, it is our great luck and our greatest burden that philosophy holds out to us the exact same opportunity, regardless of birth, gender, class, or wealth. Truly the way is open to all, though few tread these paths and fewer march confidently in a consistent direction.

"The good fortune I understand" you say, "because I see that we all have potential. But why do you say our opportunity is also a burden?"

Responsibility is both wonderful and terrible, depending on *whether you take it*. Taking responsibility for yourself and your progress gives your life meaning. Nothing makes an achievement sweeter than knowing it was hard-earned.

But look how many shirk from responsibility, from the consequences of their thoughts and actions. Because we live in an age of peace and prosperity, a person can choose to be idle, to be uninspired.

But to be average in your ambitions when others excel, where no one has forced your hand, is to know that you could have done more. Thus, people either willfully ignore their promise, or are weighed down by their potential.

This can be more damning to their spirits than if freedom was taken from them against their will. In the latter case, at least their lot is not their fault, and they are freed of the burden of responsibility.

Let me give you a final reason why you should be happy for your modest social origins.

Those born to privilege are surrounded by fine things in their cradle, and their tastes quickly grow accustomed to rich fare. Great is the risk they will set out on a path to maintaining their status and wealth.

How many will have cause to question whether wealth consists of things? And if they never question the wisdom of their choices, but blindly pursue prosperity, why should philosophy hold any appeal to them?

Though they amass wealth and power, they remain unsatisfied the whole while, and worst of all, do not know why.

I say the fortunate at birth are those who have few luxuries. For though they may start by fervently wishing for all they do not have, they have a better chance of realizing that happiness can be found in more places than their bank account, such as a walk on the beach, a vibrant sunset, or a meal with friends.

Because their progress is not assured, they take responsibility for their actions, and in this way find meaning.

The lessons of philosophy take root more readily in such a one because admission to this club requires only a well-ordered mind.

Be well.

# Chapter Seven

# On Cohen's Condos

We assume the prominent are thrilled with their privileges and made content thereby. But what do we know of their inner thoughts, their joys, and their worries?

I flew into JFK airport not long ago and marveled once again at the miracle of modern travel: Boarding a plane in the morning, crossing an ocean, and arriving at a new continent in the afternoon of the same day.

The speed with which we can conquer by air the distances of the globe is outdone, though, by the time dilation that occurs on reaching the ground, at least in New York.

It starts with the rush from the plane's door down endless, empty corridors to the customs hall.

The legs fairly leap after being caged for eight hours, and you are happy to stride energetically past the moving walkways. Why stand like a statue after you've been sitting immobile like a mummy in its sarcophagus?

The sunlight streams through the glass windows along the hallway, and your heart briefly soars with optimism that this time will be different.

Your face soon falls in line with your dashed hopes as you turn the final corner to see the Brownian motion of thousands of fellow travelers inching imperceptibly toward the next hurdle.

Quickly, which line is for you? Citizen, non-citizen, crew, green card holder, Global Entry ... choose wrongly and you will be forced to backtrack, letting who knows how many ahead of you in line and adding perhaps hours to your wait.

So, you run to then stand and shuffle while wondering for the 50th time whether those signs saying "Cell phone use prohibited" are really enforced.

There's a fellow traveler from your flight, and how on earth did they get so much farther ahead of you? They were sitting in the same row as you. Oh, there's another, and you stifle a secret laugh that you are far ahead of them.

Eventually, I clear customs, relieved to be spared the indignity of being fingerprinted and photographed like the potentially criminal non-citizens.

The baggage hall is one circle of hell I may circumvent, for at least today I am traveling light. With a pitying glance at those in the purgatory of lost baggage, I make my escape through the doors to freedom or, as it turns out, merely the arrivals hall.

I feel like a marathoner approaching the finishing line, for the way is lined with spectators holding up signs, each eagerly looking to catch sight of their runner: "Mr. Pletros, Marriott," "Electrolux," "Al Walheer, The Essex House."

If you were willing to assume a new identity for the afternoon you could be whisked any place you wish in leather and air conditioning.

In my case, I put my person into the care of that most venerable institution, The Yellow Cab Company.

Though I made my way from the plane's door with the alacrity of a seasoned competitor, first to the line, fastest out the gate, leaving less experienced runners far behind, the halls of JFK strain from the disgorge of disgruntled passengers.

Fast as I have been, before me waits another Amazonian line winding distantly to the taxis.

To truly understand motion that yields no progress, dear reader, get into a New York City cab at the very epitome of the oxymoron that is "rush hour."

- For hours you will sit, wondering whether your destination is nearing faster than the figure on the meter is rising.

- Many times, you will be tempted to fly your yellow cage and take to the streets by foot.

- Would that you had descended into the bowels of Jamaica Station and taken the E-train! The subway, with all its chance encounters and strange smells, at least gives you the sensation of movement.

It was while this run of thoughts ran riot through my tired brain that I looked out the window at 58th Street and spied a former home of hedge fund billionaire Steven Cohen.

Twenty-four-foot ceilings, spread over two floors, and in the news as much for its storied owner as for its views over Central Park.

Forced by an insider trading scandal to close SAC Capital Advisors, his eponymously initialed hedge fund, the firm paid the largest insider trading fine of all time at $1.8 billion.

Mr. Cohen was reduced to managing his own money, perhaps a mere $10 billion at that point. He had also reduced the $115 million selling price of his condo multiple times since putting it on the market in 2013.

The headlines reported it attracted a buyer after eight years and a 74% price cut. "Hah!" we laugh, "The brilliant trader has lost his golden touch." But read a bit further and you see the bargain price of $29.5 million is still $5.5 million above what he paid for it.

I am not writing to begrudge anyone their wealth, their acumen, or their pursuits, dear reader.

I would have you see that the breathless reporting of billionaires' mega apartments, art collections, and philanthropic contributions is a symptom of something else and a distraction from what is truly valuable.

The amount of ink spilled over the prominent hides as much as it reveals.

We assume the prominent are thrilled with their privileges and made content thereby. But what do we know of their inner thoughts, their joys and their worries?

Do you think the shuttering of SAC Capital's doors made Mr. Cohen any happier to open the doors of his Hamptons home?

It is not the painted walls of a grand villa that make one bright and happy. The riches that philosophy offers are available to all, regardless of what's in their wallet.

If you can but purchase peace of mind, you will see that you do not lack the means for any further purchase.

And moreover, you will see that you pay the cost of your things well after you've paid the price. The maintenance fee on a million-dollar condo is much more than what flows from your bank account each month!

When you think you are building a bulwark against uncertainty by piling up stacks of cash, be careful you are not building the walls of your own prison of discontent.

The condo I would have you inhabit is one entirely of your own making, and though it be free of adornment, you will spend more carefree days there than in any luxury building.

Be well.

# Chapter Eight

# On a Holiday Rental

## Sometimes progressing on the journey of life means leaving the comfort of what made us successful in the past

I have rented a beach property on a barrier island off the southern coastline. I hope to wile away there some sultry summer hours in rest and contemplation with my family. We will take a collective deep breath to catch up from this manic past year. I think also as much to gather our strength for what lies ahead.

Changes are afoot at summer's end, dear reader, not just in my own work life, but for all of us.

- My daughter switches universities and Cantons, leaving home to stay on course with the next phase of her studies.

- My son ends his apprenticeship and graduates with his certificate, also to begin new studies towards a degree.

- And my wife and I are moving house and moving

countries, leaving our adopted home of more than two decades to return to the land of our birth.

My wife and I are to become refugees in all but name, for I fear we have become strangers to the land that was once all we knew.

Every significant life change makes us into temporary strangers. We become strangers to our old habits and our old ways, even as we are not yet familiar with our new surroundings.

We will be fools for a while, not knowing how to get simple things done, embarrassed and uncomfortable in our ignorance.

Why do it then, one might reasonably ask? Why not just stay in our known environs? To grow and develop we must confront the new. It is an illusion that we maintain our position when we stand still because we run the risk of lapsing into complacency. Still water more easily stagnates.

Sometimes progressing on the journey of life means leaving the comfort of what made us successful in the past.

To stay successful in the future, we must take with us all that we have learned along life's journey. The cargo of life's lessons is not heavy if we pack it carefully about our persons.

One of the great opportunities a change offers us is to leave behind all that we no longer need. Jettison the dead weight of bad memories and bad experiences, of second-guessing and regret. Assimilate to yourself the best of all you have experienced and all you have learned, and not only will your steps be light, but you will be well prepared for your next step.

Remember that you have surmounted countless obstacles to get where you are today. Let the confidence of your past victories, your triumphs over so many struggles and worries and cares, carry you into the unknown with your head held high.

Will everything go according to plan? This I can tell you is hardly to be expected. Will you encounter new challenges and unexpected setbacks? Almost certainly. Will you overcome them? I have not the slightest doubt.

Can I tell you how you will overcome what comes your way? No, I cannot. But I am nonetheless supremely confident that you will prevail because you have all the lessons and skills that brought you to your current position.

Now in my case, we are not traveling so far for our summer rest that I have outrun my sense of the absurd. For starters, I cannot seem to outdistance my own folly, for I have fallen into the trap of reading the marketing material about the vacation properties on offer. As if this could tell me anything about what sort of environment will foster relaxation and restoration!

The greatest threat to our peace of mind lies within our own minds, and these we carry with us no matter how distantly we travel.

But there I was, dear reader, reading about houses arranged in military order by the number of bedrooms, bathrooms, and rows distant from the beach. Shocked at the geometric progression in price as properties inch closer to the shore and the surprising jumps as each bedroom gets tacked on.

After some time perusing the offerings, you could be forgiven for thinking that a home without a television in every room is akin to a prison sentence, each silent room promising the torture of temporary boredom.

"Can you believe they only have TVs in the bedrooms, dining room, and living room, and not the kitchen or bathrooms? How can I possibly evacuate my bowels if I am not accompanied by a screen before my face?"

"It is a hardship, dear, but I suppose you could take your iPad with you when the need comes upon you."

If I sound unkind, and I do to myself as well, it is because I am so disappointed to be reminded yet again that this is apparently what we want.

And it must be what we want because this is what the market offers at every turn: Private pools, spas, and furnished patios with gas grills; flat-screen TVs in every room and Wi-Fi throughout; a laundry room, a garage, and a walkway to the beach.

Tell me, dear reader, is it the warm embrace of your heated pool, the closed walls of your private gardens, and the flat screens facing your king-size beds that bring us to the seaside?

Or is it that moment when you slip off your shoes and socks near the end of the wooden slat walkway and feel the sand between your toes? When you first note the stiff breeze of the Atlantic wind across your face and the unmistakable smell of salt in the air?

Could it be upon hearing the reeds in the dunes rustling in the wind as you round the final curve and lay eyes on the ocean? Surely by the time you are out of the soft, dry sand and onto wetter and firmer ground, you will once again be on the way to grounding yourself in what's important.

To walk along the shore just above the sandpipers, who are themselves rushing to stay just ahead of each advancing wave, is to walk away from worldly cares.

With pelicans silhouetted by the setting sun, and dolphins' beaks occasionally breaking the surface, at that moment who cares whether you walked from the third row or the seventh? Whether you will return to a private pool, a community pool, or no pool at all? Yes, you may have a TV on every surface but still find that you are happiest leaving all screens dark.

It is outside in the wind and salt and sand that we will find ourselves closest to nature, and perhaps our own true natures.

And it is inside in the close confines of a family conversation that we will find satisfaction, and perhaps peace.

Be well.

# Chapter Nine

# On Living Simply

When traveling light you think carefully about what you really need and leave aside all those things that you might need. I think that is the reason I so love the practice

There is nothing that gives me greater pleasure than embarking on a journey with nothing more than what I can carry about my person and in a backpack!

There are now numerous websites devoted to traveling light, filled with one-bag travel adherents who have learned to love minimalism on the go. I can now travel for two weeks for business or pleasure, dear reader, with no more than the clothes on my back and an easy armful of items I can keep with me no matter how cramped my quarters.

I make my way in every environment, be it hot or cold, wet or dry, formal dress or beach casual. No hobo with their possessions tied in a sack flung over one shoulder ever felt so free of burdens as they pointed their shoes down the next highway.

When traveling light you think carefully about what you really need and leave aside all those things that you *might* need. I think that is the reason I so love the practice. It is good practice for the greater concern we continually face: Making distinctions about what is necessary to live a good life.

If only this small practice while traveling left more permanent lessons once home again. But in my familiar places, I find myself needing to remind myself over and over about what is important, lest I twist about in pursuit of possessions.

People will twist themselves into knots to avoid confronting a hard truth or to give themselves permission to believe something they desperately want to be true. Nowhere do we see this more than in the perennial question of possessions and wealth.

It is not just philosophers who have grappled with this question. The Bible addresses it frequently and generations of religious scholars have interpreted and re-interpreted its teachings ever since.

In a document as rich and complex as the Bible, no doubt you will find support for many propositions. Just like philosophers tied themselves in syllogistic knots by defining propositions and then letting logic twist all meaning away, so too have theologians found the Bible to contain a multitude of paradoxes to say nothing of support for competing propositions.

Here I would give you a general caution, dear reader, to never trust a researcher who starts with their conclusion and then scours their data for any means to support it.

We struggle to put this advice into practice because researchers often take pains to be crystal clear about their results while remaining opaque about their motives. And this assumes they have a clear idea of their motives, which you must also not take as a given.

Though you will find them less frequently, look for those researchers who first publish their hypotheses and make testable predictions. Then you may share their eagerness to experiment and check whether reality agrees.

But let me return to the Bible. Even though today we are far removed from being able to check any of the authors' motivations, some I will take on good faith. Thus, it is in the gospel of Matthew that we are told that Jesus said

> it is easier for a camel to go through the eye
> of a needle than for a rich man to enter the
> kingdom of God.

This was in the context of Jesus answering a young rich man's question about how he could achieve eternal life. Jesus's advice was for him to sell his possessions to give to the poor, and then to follow Jesus's teachings.

This prescription proved to be bitter medicine, as it has for striving people throughout the ages.

Amidst much truth-telling and honest acknowledgment among the faithful, there also followed a millennium of pretzel logic. Would there be a way to turn this simple advice entirely on its head? To say that riches and possessions here on earth were a sign of God's favor, confirmation that one was living a virtuous life?

Indeed, there arose a host of pastors preaching so-called prosperity theology, which teaches exactly this. If spiritual and physical realities are interconnected, the thinking goes, and we are entitled to well-being, then material wealth can be seen as a blessing from God.

The desire to believe this is so strong that adherents have managed to overlook a mountain of contradictory indications in the Bible and elsewhere.

The followers of conjoined spiritual and material wealth also seem unconcerned with the inherent contradiction that making regular donations to one's church is apparently a primary vehicle meant to bring about God's blessing.

This will no doubt bring material wealth to some, but I fear it is only to the lucky church receiving the faithful's donations. At this point, I am reminded of American Pastor Creflo Dollar's rather direct request to his congregants for $65 million so he could purchase a Gulfstream jet.

We do not need a Gulfstream jet to bring us great distances, dear reader. Of course, I am not speaking only of travel, although the lesson applies equally there.

I believe there is nothing inherently wrong with possessions, or in having possessions. The harm comes from the harm we do to ourselves and others in *pursuit* of possessions.

Having proven ourselves to be untrustworthy stewards of our most valuable possession, that of our well-ordered mind following reason, let us leave aside most external things so that we can learn to appreciate simple things.

If it takes a trip away from the comforts of home to remind us that we are not our things and that we can be happy with but few things, I say dust off your passport, load up your backpack, and head out your door!

Be well.

# Chapter Ten

# On Our Rotten Times

Just as advances and accomplishments belong to an age in history, so too do the embarrassments that the next generation takes but a few decades to clearly perceive

Have you noticed that each generation inevitably becomes convinced of two things, dear reader?

- First, they have reached the pinnacle of wisdom with current science and civilization; that their way of life and pursuits are correct and good and the one true path.

- And second, they simultaneously laugh at how their ancestors were so gullible and dangerously ignorant in so many things; while they lament that their children are both gullible and dangerously ignorant in so many things.

"Contemptible idiots behind us, and superficial fools ahead of us! Howsoever will the world survive when we are gone?"

It is not the times that give rise to such convictions. The folly is peculiar to humankind itself and so passes unbidden and unseen from generation to generation.

It is true that each generation finds a way to express its failings uniquely. Just as advances and accomplishments belong to an age in history, so too do the embarrassments that the next generation takes but a few decades to clearly perceive.

Humans are powerful in so many things but applying perspective to our *own* imperfections is not one of our inherent talents, nor do we seem to have any desire to develop it.

Is our own generation really the first to be free from error? Have we become enlightened as a whole, such that our every utterance deserves to be inscribed in the skies for all to wonder at?

Let us seek to be impartial judges and consider the evidence.

- We live in times where serious people seriously expound the idea that you can tell something important about the inside of a person by looking only at the outside of that person.

- That all of society can be explained by power, and that there is no objective reality behind power structures, only self-serving and self-perpetuating identity groups.

Consider the supposed attributes of "whiteness," which we are told have been invented and used to oppress non-white people.

- These include that whites value self-reliance, rational linear thinking, and the idea that hard work is the key to success.

- That it makes sense to plan for the future, delay gratification, and make progress.

- That we should have an action orientation and seek to master our circumstances.

Before you find yourself nodding along in agreement with the items on the list, recall that they are held out as symbols of oppression, not freedom.

Social justice movements hold out as heroes the victims of police brutality, as if somehow resisting arrest is the better example of virtuous conduct. Among the most exalted are the ones who have been martyred, and it does not seem to matter what their prior record may have been.

Mobs vandalize and burn city streets, and we call it justice. Crowds loot stores and we call it redistribution of wealth. City councils tell you they expect to see *less* crime when they defund the police and stop prosecuting offenders.

For our own parts, we fill our bellies with junk food, and we fill our heads with junk science. We buy junk products on credit and amuse ourselves with junk entertainment to tickle our ever-shortening attention spans.

We go into debt to pay for educations that fill our children's heads with dangerous nonsense. We borrow money to buy cars and houses that we don't need and can't afford.

All this brings us more sadness than satisfaction in both the pursuit and the possession.

On the national level, our politicians have elevated empty talk to a new art form. With one side of their mouths, they stoke our most base emotions and outrage.

So aroused, with our eyes burning red and our ears ringing, we do not notice when they utter out of the other side things like, "There are no limits on what we can spend and there is no consequence to running our deficit higher and higher."

As if! This is one time when future generations will look back not in amusement but in horror at the delusions we felt comfortable with, for we are burdening them with both our sins of omission as well as those we commit.

No, we would know on a moment's quiet reflection that ours is not the golden age, dear reader. At least, no more than any other age.

Despite our advancements in science, technology, health care, productivity, and more, we have spent little time in the laboratory of the human soul. For all our progress in external things, we have forgotten that the natural course of our minds inclines downward.

Stability in human societies is only ever temporary. We fail and we have never not failed.

The reason is that we have never removed our weaknesses and our vices from the equation. We have too few examples of virtuous behavior, and pay too little attention to the examples we have, for them to tip the scales in our favor.

In their hearts, people are not so easy to fool. We know when we are consuming garbage, though none admits it aloud.

We suffer in our hearts and our thoughts when we proclaim satisfaction with superficial things. These internal maladies do not remain suppressed but are expressed through ill health, depression, and turmoil in society.

Thus, we have sown the conditions for our downfall: Those who are told they are well-off are nonetheless unfulfilled and so restless and eager for change; while those who are told they are suffering are angry and mobilized to tear down the systems that have failed them.

Who will fight to preserve the good that humankind has achieved in its centuries of struggle? Who will ensure that the good humankind is capable of is not extinguished in the fire along with everything else?

In our rotten times, you cannot stand on the sidelines. You are either pouring water on the flames or you are fanning them. By your silence you let the rot spread.

By your words, do you seek to build and fortify or only tear down?

The early few may sacrifice themselves in standing up against madness, true. But if none stand, all will fall. And perhaps we will find that there are others who will stand with us to slow the fall.

Be well.

# Chapter Eleven

# On the Value of Wealth

## True wealth comes from not needing to display wealth to be happy, rather than having wealth to display

What good is excess wealth to a parent or their family? I have come to believe that parents who give everything to their children growing up are themselves selfish.

You are wondering if I am being contrary to make a point. You are right to wonder this, but I assure you I am sincere.

"But isn't the very definition of a good parent," you ask, "the one who is responsible and provides for their family to ensure they suffer no material want?"

I say this definition is incomplete and, moreover, insufficient, unless you are raising children to be permanent children, cut off from the cares of the outside world.

The true responsibility of parents is to raise their children to be capable of safely making their own way in the world, and not to remove every obstacle from their paths. This means learning to handle adversity.

Is life trouble-free for any person, regardless of their wealth?

Say a person has amassed a fortune as great as that of the robber barons of the Gilded Age. Does that mean they can now buy their way free from the envy, spite, and double-dealing of their fellow humans? Are their relationships protected against failing, their bodies immune from ailing, and their thoughts free of doubt?

Consider this: How can a child learn to handle adversity if they are never confronted with it?

"What," you say, "shall parents now let their children stumble unawares into the street to teach them the value of pain?"

Life will bring its own troubles soon enough, dear reader. We do not need to invite them in. The point is more that we should not seek to bar the door to every trouble.

Rather teach your children first by your own example that hardship can not only be endured but mastered. When you encounter your own inevitable setbacks show your children how you rise to the challenge, not only well, but willingly.

"I can see your point about the need to confront adversity" you say, "but why do you call parents who seek to provide a comfortable environment for their children selfish? How can wanting to give the best things to someone else make *you* selfish?"

Think about it and you will come to your answer. Will the child live only in the parent's household, or will they one day wish to live an independent life? What then? Will the parent tend to every need until the child has died of natural causes while the parent clings to life? No and no, and no to every circumstance where the outside world will intrude.

The principal thing a parent accomplishes by eliminating any real-world struggles is avoiding seeing their child suffer. Who benefits the most from such a sheltered environment?

Hence, I say this is the ultimate selfishness on the part of the parent, because in saving themselves pain they leave their children unprepared for life. I know that most parents would vehemently disagree, but that is to be expected. I have just called them selfish and bad parents in the same breath.

All right, let us respond to the incensed parent by asking them some questions:

"Reflect back upon your own life. Did everything go easily for you? Was everything you have now simply handed to you? What made you the person you are today? Tell me about a time that you overcame a hardship or a challenge and came out stronger for it."

Some of the most driven people became that way precisely because they were sorely challenged and survived the tests. Not only survived but emerged from their suffering stronger. You learn to confront adversity by being confronted with adversity.

This thought experiment is usually enough to quell the anger of all the thoughtful parents, which I believe is most of them. It quiets their voices because they are now reconsidering not only their approach to parenting but all they have done so far.

But you will encounter some number of others who say something like, "I earned my money through my own hard work. I am paid a lot because I deliver a lot of value, and I am worth every penny. How dare you say I should not give every advantage to my children now and allow them to reap the benefits of my labor?"

Everything in modern society supports the wealthy parent's view, dear reader, and your opponent has the weight of numbers and opinion on their side. Further, they have built their entire lives following a formula that was not of their making, but which they learned to master.

These roots run deep. By digging around the foundations like this you are questioning their values and by extension their very worth as a person. Do not expect your discussion to be easy and do not expect to be thanked for your service.

Be aware that many people are only too happy to be misled if it means they never have to confront painful truths.

Though they cannot permanently lay to rest a nagging dissatisfaction, they can temporarily silence this voice with a new car, a buying binge, or a trip to Vegas. The most you can hope for is to add weight to that persistent doubt so that in a quiet moment it gives them pause to think.

You might get this person to observe that on their travels through, say, Southeast Asia, they encountered many happy people who otherwise lived in poverty. That in fact having money is not the only path to happiness.

And if you arrive at this mutual realization, consider yourself a success and do not seek to go further. Because to a person who has money, the idea that money does not bring happiness is madness. Not only or even primarily for what it buys them, but for what having money tells them about themselves and what it tells others.

Money tells them that they have done the right things and are being rewarded. It tells them they are a good person! And by making lavish displays of wealth, money signals to others that a person is successful. We want nothing more than to be considered successful.

But happiness is intrinsic. I cannot show it on my arm like I can a Boss shirt under a Gucci suit jacket with a Rolex watch peeking out at the wrist. No, for bragging without talking, money beats happiness every time, at least in this person's mind.

Never mind if the parent has learned anything from you. If you have learned anything from me, dear reader, it is to identify the true value of things.

Do you seek to arouse envy in your fellow person or admiration? Does a person admire you for what you have or how you behave?

And will you set your value by the estimation of others, who do not know what is valuable and what is not? Or will you set your value by your own estimation of how well you lived according to your values?

True wealth comes from not needing to display wealth to be happy, rather than having wealth to display.

Be well.

# Chapter Twelve

# On Slippery Slopes

## Can you tell me now which of your indulgences let grown into vices will be your undoing, or will you tell me that you are safe from all temptation?

S ome people assert that the slippery slope argument is silly because no trend exists in isolation. For all the forces presently gathered and pushing in one direction, other forces will come into play and provide natural causes for things to slow, shift course, or even cease.

Now, I am the first one to applaud when I hear people say, "Do not look at this issue by itself but consider the larger context."

The biggest hurdle to effective problem-solving lies in focusing too narrowly on the problem we want to solve. By omitting the context, we forget that actions create reactions and that intended consequences are far more difficult to achieve than unintended consequences are to arise.

Most of all we forget that good intentions are all but irrelevant to actual outcomes. You may have had a noble goal in mind, but if you have designed a system that creates incentives that drive different outcomes you are making things worse, not better.

Those who say we should not fear the slippery slope are usually trying to do one of two things: Undermine opposition to a position they would like to see promoted; or convince themselves that their own little indulgences are acceptable.

I'll leave for another day the discussion of this topic as applied to politics and law, interesting though it is. Right now, dear reader, I want to address your question of whether we must be so strict in denying ourselves pleasures and so rigorous in casting out negative emotions.

In other words, are we as people standing on slippery slopes, or do we have ourselves under control?

The highest state of mind, well-ordered and applying reason to each situation, will place the proper value on emotions and guide our judgment and actions.

There is no reason at all not to take pleasure in the things that are necessary for life. One of the goals of our practice is to learn to live a good life, and surely enjoying life is part of that practice.

Similarly, there is no doubt that emotions are part of what it means to be human. To suggest otherwise is to place unreasonable expectations on any person; we are not robots!

No indeed, but just as we are no mere machines, so have few of us achieved that state of having perfect wisdom in all things. We are tempted and we are easily led astray. What begins as a simple indulgence can grow into the greatest of monsters, devouring far in excess of reasoned appetite.

"Yes, that happens" you say, "but must it happen every time with every person? Can't I be trusted to safely manage the smallest of my daily affairs?"

Do you think I exaggerate the dangers once again, dear reader? Consider for a moment how many ways humans can become addicted. It is easy enough to see that most vices start as harmless pleasures no one could argue against in isolation.

- For one group, it is an occasional drink, a cigarette, or watching a few YouTube videos.

- Another group might be tempted by a spot of online shopping, giving in to a twinge of jealousy, or giving vent to a bout of anger.

- Yet another puts a few dollars on fantasy football, takes a flutter at the track, or wants to bet whether the ball will land on red this time.

For each of them, you can say "No harm done, and anyway, those are not my vices. I like a piece of chocolate, placing my bets not in Vegas but on stocks, and leasing a new car every so often. I can afford it and have handled myself without a problem so far. So really, what is the harm?"

Here is how that sounds to me, dear reader. No different than the person who says "I enjoy a glass of wine or a beer in the evening every now and then. What harm of it?"

And they would be right, in most cases, just as you are right. But even when this person's periodic drink becomes a daily drink, you will find them saying "I am in control. I can stop anytime I want. I drink because I want to, not because I have to." We all know where such self-talk has led too many people.

Can you tell me now which of your indulgences let grown into vices will be your undoing, or will you tell me that you are safe from all temptation?

If so, you must also explain to me how it is that the rolls of the Anonymous organizations number so many millions. I am speaking of Alcoholics Anonymous, Gambling Anonymous, Narcotics Anonymous, and the like.

A staggering number of both substances and behaviors generate addictive behavior. From alcohol, opioids, and nicotine, to gambling, gaming, and shopping. You will be thinking but perhaps hesitant to point out that working and exercise addiction afflicts some as well, and you would be right.

And this just scratches the surface.

You know I like to look beneath the surface, so let's do so together. Humans by their nature are designed to seek out pleasurable experiences — food, sex, relaxation — because these things help ensure we survive and procreate.

We can indulge pleasures more safely in times of scarcity because there is little danger then of their becoming vices. But when we can get what we want whenever we want, the danger of overindulgence becomes great.

Things that are good in moderation do not remain so in excess. But there is no reliable guide to tell us when enough becomes too much.

When it is within our power to self-dose, we should be most mistrustful of our ability to find the limit, because it is blurred by the pleasure of the moment. And once in the grip of an indulgence turned to vice, it is far harder to extricate ourselves from its clutches.

The safest course is to never start down the road of idle pleasures.

If I cannot convince you it is safer to forego pleasures altogether, at a minimum you must set yourself guidelines in advance.

For each pleasure you give yourself indulgence to pursue, do not leave your judgment to the time when you are under their influence. When you are of sound mind, decide your limit in all things, and decide to listen to your mind.

Try this method first in small things to see if you can trust yourself. In this way, you may build up habits of self-preservation that keep you from falling all the way down the slope.

Be well.

# Chapter Thirteen

# On Stepping Off the Treadmill

Can we be trusted to treat equally the good luck and bad luck that comes our way, because neither perturbs the reasoning of our well-ordered minds?

A bout ten years after I started working in-house, I was gripped by a yawning uncertainty. It was that a great deal of the time my team and I were spending was wasted on tasks of little importance and no ultimate impact.

Nothing is more damaging to motivation than to think that you are running flat out but making no progress. In the legal team's case, it was churning through hundreds and thousands of contracts, negotiating the same damage limitation clauses over and over, to no real effect.

It is certainly good to be confident in what you are doing because self-doubt is destructive of peace of mind. But it is better to first be self-critical and to reflect on what you are doing.

Although this questioning is initially uncomfortable, careful thinking gives rise to well-founded conclusions about the wisdom of what you are doing. Bolstered by the assurance of the correctness of your actions, you can tackle any task and overcome any hurdle.

The hours we spend working are not just mindless toil, undermined by the worry that it is also meaningless toil. The work is noble, purposeful, and of our own choosing.

This line of thinking is what causes me to react strongly, dear reader, to some of the more superficial questions we are confronted with.

We have set our lives to the important task of learning to live well. Of what use are word games and trifles, pursuits that distract and amuse us but do not give us any useful weapons to take into combat? I want the answers not just to hard questions and paradoxes for the sake of solving a puzzle, but for learning what to do and what not to do, and why.

- We will be put in terrible situations of pain and suffering. Can we learn not to needlessly suffer, and add to our burdens with burdens made of our own thinking?

- We will be tempted with riches and wonders and given the chance to pursue the same shiny things all our fellows seek. Will we have acquired in our studies the wisdom to respond with as much care to the favors of Fortune as we do to the evils that surround us?

- Can we be trusted to treat equally the good luck and bad luck that comes our way, because neither perturbs the reasoning of our well-ordered minds?

I say we are at greater risk than the average person by virtue of our studies.

"Why is this" you ask? "Are we not better armed by virtue of our careful work? How can the study of philosophy be of use if it only puts me in greater danger?"

The risk of harm comes about precisely because we have learned to avoid many pitfalls. In particular, we have learned to apply the power of continuous improvement to many situations. This means we will experience steady progress and success in many areas of our lives.

- If you wish to pursue wealth, you will be more likely than most to attain it. For achieving material wealth is not intrinsically hard if you apply the right systems and mindset.

- Ironically, the person who learns to be happy with little is likely to be blessed with many small surpluses. Set prudently aside these small gains can easily grow into greater wealth.

Our greater danger does not go uncompensated, dear reader. For one, we are given weapons against the many accidents and insults that life will confront us with. Being prepared for adversity is a most worthy addition to our armory.

And for another, the dangers I am describing come from being showered with successes. Few of our fellow humans would view that as much of a problem.

And exactly therein lies the problem. We remain vigilant because we know that the saying "Success begets success" does not apply universally.

Indeed, I would say that for all but those who are disciplined of mind and in firm possession of their reason, the saying should be "Success begets dissatisfaction."

How many powerful people do you know who, having attained a certain position in an organization, say "I am content where I am. I need nothing more."? How many wealthy people eschew accumulating additional wealth?

And to make the case more generally and more damningly, perhaps the saying should be "Success begets disillusionment." How many people who, having attained a goal they sought most assiduously, value it the same upon reaching it as they did while seeking it?

Far more typical is to say, "It's not what I thought," or worse, to not think about it at all because they have their sights set on the next prize.

For all the celebrities, millionaires, and social media stars that the masses look upon in envy, how many do you think repose in complete satisfaction? Not the self-satisfaction of pampered ease, but genuine satisfaction at their lot in life. Not needing anything external, not wanting anything they do not have, not wishing to be relieved of a burden they are carrying.

You need only look to the carrying on when one of them suffers a public setback to know that their supposed happiness is only skin deep.

I tell you, do not seek to trade places with any person no matter how fortunate they seem to you. For all the visible signs of their success you may be gaining, you are also inheriting their fears, their worries, and their unchecked desires. And who knows if they have half your ability to control themselves.

Take uncomplainingly what comes your way, good or bad and, yes, work steadily towards improving your situation.

But do not make the attainment of external possessions your aim, or you are stepping on a treadmill that is constantly running. This treadmill will make a runner out of you to be sure, but the work serves only to exhaust and wear you down, not to make you more fit.

In contrast, the measured steps you take after careful reflection are much more likely to take you in a direction of your choosing and which will therefore be more to your liking.

Be well.

# Chapter Fourteen

# A Little Philosophy Goes a Long Way

In our journey to finding happiness, thinking for ourselves is the key to unlocking and then banishing all the bad habits that may have crept into our lives

T he best reward for sharing Stoic lessons is the sincere hope they will help you and others live good lives.

Two letters in the series provide a summary and a powerful incentive to pursue the lessons Stoicism offers us, so I'll give you a brief recap here.

In *Thinking for Yourself*, we discuss why some types of nonconformism are good.

While we are rightly critical of unthinking rebellion, or fighting the system for the sake of it, that is not what Stoicism expects. Stoicism asks us to challenge blind conformity to the current system, i.e. doing what everyone else does without questioning the underlying values of what everyone is doing.

The Stoic's task is initially the harder one: Taming one's passions and desires is a greater challenge than looking to change others. But the reward in determining the proper value of things is greater. The Stoic finds happiness by putting it firmly under the control of their reason.

Thankfully, we don't need to address all our needs at once. We make the most progress by taking little steps consistently. Here's what *Thinking for Yourself* tells us:

"My advice is to consider every day as a session in the classroom of life. I feel confident in predicting that on most days you will be confronted with inconveniences, annoyances, or irritants. The varieties are endless.

By applying your reason, you will put each stimulus in its proper place, and you will not be put out of sorts against your will. Either there is some validity to the thing that irks you or there is none.

- In the first case, you have been given an opportunity to better yourself.

- In the latter case, you have been given an opportunity to practice placing the true value on things.

- Over time it becomes easier to distinguish false harms and, so identified, they lose their ability to hurt you. Or better said, you stop inflicting harm on yourself.

The same mechanisms that trick us into adopting bad habits allow us to give up those habits. If doing something regularly for a few weeks makes it habit-forming, then not doing it for a few weeks also becomes habit-forming.

This sounds so trivial as to be useless, but I tell you it transformed my life. My iron willpower is nothing more than the accumulation of little habits, including refraining from things that I have targeted for extinction.

I use my reason to determine the deeper value of things and to think for myself. The main thing I am trying to uncover is what makes me unhappy, so I can do it less. At the same time, I hypothesize about what will make me happy, so I can do it more."

Thus, in our journey to finding happiness, thinking for ourselves is the key to unlocking and then banishing all the bad habits that may have crept into our lives.

In *Reason of the Well-Ordered Mind*, we start with a reminder of why we study philosophy at all:

"We are conducting our studies for a purpose. If we have resolved not to be idle, and even in our free time to obtain some good for ourselves, then surely it is for the aim of living good lives.

Not in the future, or at some point when we will have attained a more perfect state. Right now, today and every day. We have but one life and what a shame it is to be living unhappy or, worse, to be living in a form of suspended animation."

And we conclude by describing how one attains the desired state of living a good life:

What can bring about this state? It is the same thing that disturbs it, namely our minds.

We mistakenly place the blame on external things, but this is an illusion that we can penetrate by careful contemplation. Thus,

our highest purpose is to order our minds so that we can follow
reason in all things."

I will end with one of my favorite gems of advice from Seneca
himself. It is a lesson that bears repeating because so much of
modern life pulls us in other directions and causes us to forget:

> Set yourself free for your own sake; gather and
> save your own time. While we are postponing,
> life speeds by.

Be well.

www.ingramcontent.com/pod-product-compliance
Lightning Source LLC
Chambersburg PA
CBHW060351050426
42449CB00011B/2927